Crayola

CRAYOLA COLORS OF CANADA

Mari Schuh

Lerner Publications ◆ Minneapolis

For Brody, Brianne, Madison, and Kellen

Content consultant: Shannon Zila, Child Advocate and Early Childhood Administrator, Member of the Blackfoot Nation

Lerner Publications Company
An imprint of Lerner Publishing Group, Inc.
241 First Avenue North
Minneapolis, MN 55401 USA

For reading levels and more information, look up this title at www.lernerbooks.com.

Main body text set in Mikado Medium.
Typeface provided by HVD Fonts.

Library of Congress Cataloging-in-Publication Data

Names: Schuh, Mari C., 1975– author.
Title: Crayola colors of Canada / by Mari Schuh.
Description: Minneapolis : Lerner Publications, 2020. | Series: Crayola country colors | Audience: Grades K–3. | Audience: Age 5–9. | Includes bibliographical references and index.
Identifiers: LCCN 2019016935 (print) | LCCN 2019017558 (ebook) | ISBN 9781541582699 (eb pdf) | ISBN 9781541572669 (lb : alk. paper) | ISBN 9781541587137 (pb : alk. paper)
Subjects: LCSH: Canada—Juvenile literature. | Colors—Juvenile literature. | Crayons—Juvenile literature.
Classification: LCC F1008.2 (ebook) | LCC F1008.2 .S36 2020 (print) | DDC 971—dc23

LC record available at https://lccn.loc.gov/2019016935

Manufactured in the United States of America
1-46533-47578-8/21/2019

TABLE OF CONTENTS

LET'S VISIT CANADA! 4

LOOKING AROUND 6

COLORFUL CREATURES 10

CELEBRATIONS 16

More about Canada!   20
Many Colors   21
Glossary   22
To Learn More   23
Index   24

LET'S VISIT CANADA!

Canada is a beautiful, colorful country.

It is in North America.

Let's explore the colors of Canada!

LOOKING AROUND

Canada has clear **blue** lakes and **bright green** forests.

The sun shines on tall, jagged mountains.

Golden sunlight
fills the big,
wide sky.

Water rushes down Niagara Falls.

White mist fills the air.

COLORFUL CREATURES

Blue jays live in the forest.

They look for fruit, nuts, seeds, and bugs to eat.

Black-and-white puffins leave the water to lay eggs.

This puffin picks a **purple** flower for its nest.

A red fox
hunts alone.

Black, white, and **red-orange** fur keeps it warm.

Beluga whales swim in Canada's ocean waters.

These whales are born **gray** or **brown**.

Their skin turns white as they get older.

CELEBRATIONS

People in Canada celebrate National Indigenous Peoples Day.

They celebrate the cultures and histories of Canada's native peoples.

The traditional outfits of the indigenous peoples have many beautiful colors.

People wear **red** and **white** on Canada Day!

This holiday is July 1.

It honors the day that Canada became a country.

MORE ABOUT CANADA!

Continent: North America
Capital city: Ottawa
Population: 35,881,659 (July 2018 est.)

ARCTIC OCEAN

Canada

NORTH AMERICA

ATLANTIC OCEAN

ASIA

EUROPE

PACIFIC OCEAN

AFRICA

PACIFIC OCEAN

SOUTH AMERICA

INDIAN OCEAN

AUSTRALIA

SOUTHERN OCEAN

MANY COLORS

There are so many colors in Canada. Here are some of the Crayola® crayon colors used in this book.

BLUE VIOLET

BLUSH

DANDELION

BRICK RED

GLOSSARY

beluga: a species of toothed whale

cultures: the ways of life of different groups of people

holiday: a special day of celebration

indigenous peoples: the original inhabitants of an area or country

mist: a cloud of tiny drops of water in the air

native: originally belonging to a certain place or country

Niagara Falls: waterfalls on the border of the US and Canada

North America: the continent that includes Canada, the US, Mexico, and Central America

TO LEARN MORE

Books

Blevins, Wiley. *Canada*. New York: Scholastic, 2018.

Dean, Jessica. *Canada*. Minneapolis: Pogo, 2019.

Parkes, Elle. *Let's Explore Canada*. Minneapolis: Lerner Publications, 2018.

Websites

Canada Flag Coloring Page
https://www.crayola.com/free-coloring-pages/print/canada-flag-coloring-page/

National Geographic Kids: Canada
https://kids.nationalgeographic.com/explore/countries/canada/

INDEX

Canada Day, 18

celebrate, 16

color, 4, 5, 17

forests, 6, 10

National Indigenous
  Peoples Day, 16

Niagara Falls, 9

North America, 4

water, 9, 11

PHOTO ACKNOWLEDGMENTS

Image credits: Pierre Leclerc/Shutterstock.com, p. 1; Radius Images/Getty Images, p. 4 (northern lights); Creative Travel Projects/Shutterstock.com, p. 4 (leaves); TerenceLeezy/Moment/Getty Images, p. 4 (bear); benedek/E+/Getty Images, p. 5 (city); LWA/The Image Bank/Getty Images, p. 5 (hockey); nurserowan/iStock/Getty Images, pp. 6–7; mrclark321/iStock/Getty Images, p. 9; FotoRequest/Shutterstock.com, p. 10; mlorenzphotography/Moment/Getty Images, p. 11; David Kalosson/Shutterstock.com, p. 12; W6/iStock/Getty Images, p. 15; Steve Russell/Toronto Star/Getty Images, p. 16; Mark Spowart/Alamy Stock Photo, p. 17; VisualCommunications/iStock/Getty Images, p. 19; Laura Westlund/Independent Picture Service, p. 20 (map); Pgiam/E+/Getty Images, p. 20 (flag).

Cover: Joannis S Duran/Moment/Getty Images (fireworks); Lily Marcheterre/iStock/Getty Images (landscape); RT Images/Shutterstock.com (fox); outdoorsman/Shutterstock.com (polar bears).